Early Schools

Bobbie Kalman

The Early Settler Life Series

Crabtree Publishing Company

www.crabtreebooks.com

To Marc, our budding, brilliant photographer

A very special thanks to the following people without whose help this book would not have been possible:

Lise Gunby, who was invaluable to me in researching, writing, and designing this book.

My excellent editorial and art staff: *Nancy Cook* and *Rosemary McLernon*.

The skilled photographers who are responsible for the faithful reproductions of historical materials: *Sarah Peters* and *Stephen Mangione*.

The historians and librarians who provided me with research and photographic opportunities: *Richard Schofield, William Loos, Margaret Crawford Maloney, Dana Tenny, Jill Shefrin, Lynne Kurylo.*

Cataloging in Publication Data

Kalman, Bobbie, 1947 –
  Early Schools

(Early settler life series)
Includes index.
ISBN   0–86505–015–5 hardcover
ISBN   0–86505–014–7 softcover

1. Education – History.   2. Schools – History.
I. Title.   II. Series.

LA 128. K 33   370. 9   LC 93-27359

PMB 16A
350 Fifth Avenue, Suite 3308
New York, NY 10118

612 Welland Avenue
St. Catharines,
Ontario Canada L2M 5V6

73 Lime Walk
Headington, Oxford OX3 7AD
United Kingdom

Contents

When the settlers arrived in the new land, there were no schools. Those who wanted their children to read or learn arithmetic had to teach them at home. Father and son do their best to figure out a difficult arithmetic problem. Father is puzzled and scratches his head. His son has given up!

Too busy for book-learning

Education was a luxury that the earliest settlers could not afford. There was too much work to be done. Trees had to be cut down. The land had to be cleared. Houses and barns had to be built. Crops had to be planted so that the settlers would have food. Who had time for book-learning? There were many other lessons that had to be learned. The most important subjects to know about were the soil, planting times, how to store food, and where to find fresh water. To understand Latin, Greek, arithmetic, and grammar did not seem useful. Even settlers who had gone to school in their homelands discovered that building a new life by hand did not leave much time for the mind.

As people became more established, they realized that book-learning could be useful too. How could you keep accounts in a store if you knew nothing about arithmetic? How could you sign land deeds unless you had learned to write? It was easier to keep up with outside events if you could read church notices or a newspaper. As life in the new communities became more complicated, people realized that it was easier to do well if you could read and write.

Read the story, *To build or not to build*, to learn how one community arrived at its decision to build the first schoolhouse.

4

To build or not to build

Everyone in the village, from old Gramps Shawcross down to little Alma Shawcross, had crowded into the general store. Gramps held a special place in the community. He had been the first settler in the area, and the first to become a great-grandfather. His family had given its name to Shaw's Crossing.

The previous Sunday, the minister had announced that he was inviting everyone in the community to a meeting on Monday to discuss the possibility of opening a local schoolhouse. Everybody was eager to attend. Mr. Campbell had piled his supplies against the walls of his store to make room for all the people. They waited impatiently for Doctor Duncan because he would bring along Mr. Whitney, the young man who was offering to teach in the village.

The minister arrived looking as serious as he did on Sundays. He had the doctor in tow, who was followed in turn by a young man. The minister stopped at the store counter. "Neighbors," he said, "let me introduce Mr. Whitney, an enthusiastic young English fellow who'd appreciate the opportunity to open a school in our district. Now you all know our own Doctor Duncan. He's volunteered to say a few words about Mr. Whitney."

The doctor gives his diagnosis

Doctor Duncan stepped forward. He paused, greatly pleased with the hush that suddenly blanketed the room. "I was born into this community," he began, "and am proud to call myself a native of Shaw's Crossing. I know you all, and you all know me. You also know I've said many times that it's time our village supported its own real school. We've had the benefit of lessons given in the church by our good minister, and we've made do with our dame school. In fact," he added hastily after catching the eagle eye of Mrs. Shawcross, "Mrs. Shawcross has done a fine job with our little ones in her dame school. But times are changing, and our little ones keep getting bigger but don't have any higher classes to move on to." The doctor looked out the corner of his eye at Mrs. Shawcross.

Her feathers were obviously ruffled. Mrs. Shawcross was the widowed daughter of Gramps. She was a plump, gray-haired woman with spectacles perched on her nose. She was about fifty years old. The dame school had been run in her home for a quarter of a century, ever since her young husband was killed in a farming accident. She taught the children while she sewed and knitted. They recited while she worked with her hands. Between the small sums that her students' parents paid when they could afford to, and the money she made selling her handiwork, Mrs. Shawcross lived comfortably. She was not at all pleased with these new-fangled ideas about education.

Mrs. Shawcross defends her dame school

"Doctor Duncan," she now said, drawing out the syllables in his name, "I too am a long-standing member of this community. I am now teaching my second generation of youngsters. I myself was taught by my mother. She did a fine job, and I, if I may say so myself, do a finer. Now this young man thinks he can replace me."

Mrs. Shawcross looks like a sweet little Grandma, but Jack did not get away with telling a lie in her dame school!

Mr. Gee teaches his son at home. John is learning to become a blacksmith too. He knows how to read a little from the Bible. However, he also needs to learn arithmetic in order to keep the business books. Mr. Gee realizes that some schooling may help his son after all.

"Mrs. Shawcross," interrupted the doctor, "my dear Mrs. Shawcross. No one here is disputing your ability to carry on a fine school. As a matter of fact, I'm sure Mr. Whitney would be grateful for your advice and assistance should he establish himself here. We could never do without you, Mrs. Shawcross."

The argument heats up

The dame's feathers were smoothed, but Mr. Gee, the blacksmith, had his own objection. "I need my boy in my shop," he hammered out in one-syllable words, "and all he needs to know is how to hold steady a big horse and drive nails at the same time. He doesn't need your fancy books. He needs to know his numbers so he can keep the shop's business straight."

Mr. Whitney had thought it wiser to let the doctor speak for him, but now he raised his hand to get the attention of the crowd. "Mr. Gee," he said respectfully, "I don't plan to start a fancy school which would be unsuitable for Shaw's Crossing. I'd be happy to teach how to keep books as well as read them, and certainly a little writing wouldn't hurt."

Mr. Gee grumbled a bit, but figured addition and letters might not be so bad.

Lessons learned from the land

Ben Moss wasn't going to change his mind that easily. He owned a farm a few kilometers away, and he needed his five sons to help work it. He had come from England to build a homestead eighteen years earlier. He had cleared his land, put up fences, and built a house. He still remembered the first day his plow had turned the soil that had never been farmed before - not since the beginning of time! That moment when his plow bit into the earth was a symbol to Ben of his accomplishment in the new country. Whenever he thought of it he felt proud. He wanted to give his sons the same feeling.

"I'm not so good at saying what I mean," he said, "but I think lessons should be learned from the land, the hard but right way. My sons need to know when to plant and when to sow, as it says in the Bible. They need to judge crops and livestock. I can't have my boys spend all day away from their proper jobs. They'll learn silly old Latin and forget the land."

"Ben," answered the doctor, "all five of your boys can't farm your land when they're married with families. Shaw's Crossing needs fine boys like yours to become teachers and doctors. We need leaders in this village and in this country, not followers. And school," he added gently, "might teach your sons to feel that they can put their ideas about living into words."

"We can't afford a school!"

Ben wasn't fooled by flattery, but he did know his boys were fine and deserved the best. Before he could speak again, his neighbor, Mrs. Reed, chimed in: "My girls don't need book-learning either. Girls should learn to keep house. They need spinning and cooking lessons. I can teach them what they need to know. They have to keep bread on the table, and they can only do that by making it from scratch! Besides, we can't afford a schoolhouse!" Some of the people muttered in agreement. The minister stopped them. "Mr. Whitney has agreed to teach for the sum of one cent a day per pupil if you all agree to provide firewood," he said. The amount seemed a fair price. At least it silenced some of the mutterers.

Gramps makes a speech

Gramps Shawcross had been sitting quietly at the back. Now he stood and raised his cane for quiet.

"I've been listening to you all put in your two cents worth when all Mr. Whitney asks is one cent and a chance." There were a few chuckles at his little joke. He continued, "I'm an old man. I've seen

this village grow from a crossroads until it wouldn't be exaggerating to call it a town. When I first came, a handshake sealed a bargain and there was no need for putting words on paper to make a contract between friends and neighbors. I know I'm not ashamed that I can only sign an "X". Nobody taught me to read or write. I know I've worked awfully hard all my life. I have my doubts about handing children books when they ought to be handling tools."

"But times are changing, as you say, Doc, and Mr. Whitney here tells me today that most other towns already have schoolhouses. My wife, she could read, and she taught my daughter. She'd have a chart of the letters on the kitchen wall and drill her while she baked and washed. Young Mrs. Shawcross here, why, she could recite Bible verses enough to make your head spin when she was four years old. And my wife, bless her soul, she brought something kind of special to those times when we did rest from work. She'd read to me many an evening."

From crossroads to community

"Between the good work of my daughter and the minister and all you parents and grandparents who take the children in hand, we've made do here," Gramps said. "But it's time to work out something permanent. We're a community now, not a crossroads, and so we ought to share in building a school just like we share our help and supplies."

"My friends and neighbors here don't all seem so eager about this school business, but maybe we can make a go of it with Mr. Whitney's help."

Gramps turned to the crowd. A few still looked rebellious, but most were nodding and smiling. Little Alma was sniffling, but only because she was hungry and tired of all these people. He turned to Mr. Whitney, and in the sternest voice but with the biggest smile, he said to the new school-teacher, "You've got the job, it seems, but see you don't teach too darn much Latin. My part of the bargain is that I'll give you the wood and Shawcross land. That is," he said, "if the rest of you will lend your hearts and hands for the building."

Shaw's Crossing finally opens its school. The building is not very fancy, but it is better than no school at all. The villagers are proud of their work.

Education, a community effort

Before there was a school or a teacher, children were sometimes taught by the minister in the village church.

We see from the story of Shaw's Crossing that there were other ways of teaching before schoolhouses were built and school-teachers hired. Children learned from parents and grandparents. Young children might be sent to dame schools such as the one run by Mrs. Shawcross. They did not learn very much. Most of their time was spent memorizing Bible passages and reciting them to the dame as she worked at her sewing or knitting.

Sometimes ministers held classes in their churches. In some areas, however, the school was built before the church, so church services were held in the classroom. In some villages and towns, the minister and teacher were the same person, and a small school was erected beside the church.

Schoolhouses were not among the first buildings to appear in the community. More important to the settlers were their houses, barns, and fences. The settlers shared tools, supplies, and skills. They worked together to build a community. Once the community started to develop, then they could find the time and energy to build a schoolhouse to benefit everyone.

Not all of these children are happy to be going to school. Some find book-learning more difficult than working at home. Having to sit still for so many hours is no easy task. On top of it all, you have to pay attention to the teacher! Some of the children would rather be fishing at the millpond.

All the children in this old photograph were taught in one room. Some were as young as five years old. Some were close to twenty. The teacher had a hard job. He could not teach everyone at once. He had to prepare several different lessons.

The first schoolhouses

Schools were built on land that was not suitable for farming. The settlers usually chose some land near the crossroads of the community. The school yard often had no trees. There was no shade from the heat in summer. The winds whistled through the building in winter. Children sat huddled together in order to keep warm. Sometimes it was so cold that the ink froze in the inkwells.

Dirt floors and paper windows

The first schoolhouses were made of logs. They had dirt floors. The windows were covered with greased paper instead of glass. Lard rubbed into the paper made it transparent. Later schools had windows, but they were quickly broken by the students. Often there was no money for repairs. Rags were stuffed into the openings in the windows to keep out the cold.

Dangling legs

There were no single desks in the early schoolhouses. The children sat on benches at narrow tables. There was no support for their backs. The students often faced the walls because the table tops were built into them. The smaller students sat on benches and had to dangle their feet because their little legs were too short to reach the floor.

Too hot or too cold

The earliest schoolrooms were heated by a smoky fire. The children close to the fire were too hot, and those who sat far from it froze. In later days there were stoves, but the students still had the same problems. The heat was not spread evenly throughout the room.

This old picture shows an 1810 classroom. It is made of logs. The benches are built right into the walls. The teacher must sit on an uncomfortable stool. A fireplace made of logs heats the room in winter.

The schoolmaster is very strict. He often gives his students a good caning. This poor student fell asleep during the lesson. The teacher has yanked him off the bench by his collar. Will this just be a warning? The other students seem to enjoy the poor boy's misery. However, they must not be too happy when it is their turn to be at the receiving end of that long stick!

It is Anna's turn to start the school fire this morning. She must get to the school before the others. She takes kindling wood with her so the fire will heat up quickly.

Keeping the school fire burning

Finding enough firewood was a big problem for the students and their teacher. In the winter, the fire or stove was the only way to keep the schoolhouse warm. It seemed that there was never enough wood to burn.

Each winter, parents were supposed to bring a load of firewood for every child they sent to school. When they did not, their children suffered. In the first place, they froze. Secondly, some teachers expelled the children of the guilty parents or made them sit in the coldest part of the room. In some towns, parents were fined if they did not bring firewood.

One student was assigned the task of starting the fire each frosty morning. The pupil with this job had to get the fire going before the other students arrived. If he or she was late, the little children cried and complained and the teacher shouted. Often it was so cold that the children wore their outdoor clothes inside.

Hiking or hitching?

There was no such thing as a school bus in the early days. Children walked to school. Some had to walk miles with bare feet. The cold was often bitter. The luckier children had shoes or hitched rides with their father or neighbors. A few even had their own horses, which they tied up in the school yard.

Bareback and barefoot!

These settler girls set out on their long walk to school. They have no shoes. Their lunch is tied up in a rag.

Priscilla walks to school in the spring and fall. She loves the winter because she can ride to school in style. Her pet goat, Miranda, pulls her in the tiny cutter.

These children were lucky to go to a school that provided a school bus. The driver made the rounds each morning picking up all the students in the neighborhood. They are now returning home after a hard day at school.

This old schoolroom shows how little teachers and students had to work with. The tables are rough and narrow. All the students must face the wall. There is one blackboard, a map, a bell, a few books, and slates. No wonder the teacher has problems keeping the attention of her pupils. One of her disobedient students is being punished by missing recess. However, the teacher is the one who suffers. She surely could use a break.

Homemade school supplies

There was no sophisticated equipment at the earliest schools. Most lessons were written on a slate with chalk. Paper was expensive. Paper was so precious that at some schools students wrote on birch bark instead. When parents could afford to buy their children paper, the only kind available was rough and dark. The children then had to make their own notebooks. They folded the paper twice to make four leaves or eight pages and covered the book with wrapping paper. One edge was sewed so that the book was bound. The children even had to draw their own lines for ruled paper.

Before lead pencils were invented, pupils used pens or charcoal for all of their

paperwork. The pens were made of goose quills. One of the schoolmaster's most important jobs was to mend and sharpen them.

Each family made its own ink. The children brought it with them to school. They used ink powder that they had bought at the store and mixed with water. Poor families in the country, who could not afford ink powder, used the bark of the swamp maple tree to make their ink. They boiled the bark in a kettle to make a black liquid, and then added a chemical called *copperas* to make the liquid thicker. Homemade ink was not very good and it often dried up.

Stephen's parents cannot afford to buy him paper. He is disappointed because he knows the answer to the teacher's question. He scratches it into his desk in protest.

Eve teaches Ann her letters, using a quill pen and ink. The girls are lucky to have these luxuries.

Beware!

Children were very careful not to lose their books. If they did, they probably would not get new ones. The child who wrote this poem in the front of his book warned thieves to watch out!

> Whosoever steals this
> Book away may
> Think on that great
> judgement day when
> Jesus Christ shall
> come and say
> Where is that book you
> stole away.
> Then you will say
> I do not know
> and Christ will say
> go down below.

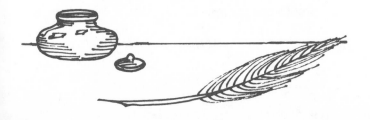

Most children did their school work on slates. This boy can rub off his work of art in the blink of an eye. If the teacher sees his picture, the boy will be in trouble.

Mr. Plunkett has the best seat in the schoolhouse. He can warm his feet by the stove.

A long school day

Peter and Dorothy attend a one-room country school. It is eight o'clock in the morning and they are starting on their hour-long walk from home to the schoolhouse. It is winter time, and they are bundled up so tightly that they can hardly move. They have been awake for hours, Dorothy churning butter and Peter helping Father fix a fence that the cows had trampled during the night. But they set off with their homemade copybooks and the readers that were hand-me-downs from older cousins. This year Dorothy is quite proud because she has her very own feather quill and ink bottle. Peter is a little jealous. He uses a slate and chalk.

By the time they arrive the tips of Peter's ears are frostbitten, but neither Dorothy nor Mr. Plunkett, the teacher, give him much sympathy. They suffer from chilblains, so their hands and feet are swollen. The only warm place in the room is by the stove, and Mr. Plunkett usually takes the best seat where he can warm his poor old feet by the fire.

Ready, stand, step, and kneel!

Dorothy and Peter arrive just in time for the opening exercises. The bell rings and the class marches in single file into the school and into their seats. Mr. Plunkett reads a Bible passage about honoring Father and Mother and then the class kneels to say the Lord's Prayer. The teacher tells the students when to stand and kneel by ringing the bell on his desk. The first bell means "get ready." When the second bell rings, everyone stands. Bell three means everyone must step into the aisles. And when the fourth bell rings – get down on your knees!

Next Mr. Plunkett reads the roll call. Daniel Brown is missing again and Mr. Plunkett always locks out latecomers. Somehow Daniel manages not to freeze. Late pupils are allowed in after recess.

Letters backwards and forwards

The first class is reading and writing. The students are divided into four groups of two grades each. Each group has a reader. Peter is in his third year and second reader. While Mr. Plunkett listens to the young ones recite the alphabet forwards and backwards (and then backwards without looking!), the older pupils copy from their readers. Their handwriting is beautiful! Then the higher grades recite while the lower grades carefully copy their letters.

Geography class is at ten o'clock. The poor students have to memorize the names of countries, lakes, rivers, and mountains. They use a big globe on a stand which Mr. Plunkett twirls so fast that all the colors run together.

Figuring it out

Arithmetic is next. Each class figures out problems on slates. Afterwards, the classes are drilled. They have to add, subtract, multiply, and divide out loud without writing anything down. No one volunteers. When students raise their hands, they had better be very sure they can answer quickly and correctly. Mr. Plunkett gives no points for just trying - you have to succeed. The students wait until he points at them with his long stick. They rise, trembling all over. Jack Johnson has trouble with arithmetic. Every other day he is crowned with the dunce cap and sent to the corner.

Recess after geography

After geography there is a ten-minute recess. By the time the students put on all their winter clothes they have only a few minutes outside. On the way in they are allowed to take a drink from the bucket of water by the door. Today it is Peter's turn to bring in firewood for the stove.

Spelling out loud

After eating lunch, which the children bring in pails, it is time for grammar. Grammar lessons begin as soon as the children learn to read, and continue until they leave school. Hardly anybody likes grammar. Some even prefer spelling! The early grades spell aloud words written on the blackboard. The later grades have drills. They scribble furiously to keep up with Mr. Plunkett, who delights in racing his own students. Every Friday afternoon the school holds a spelling match. Believe it or not, it is the most exciting part of the week!

The last lesson is oral reading. It is very important to be able to make a good speech. Even the small students manage to stutter out a few lines. Mr. Plunkett does have a kind streak, however, and he sometimes lets the little ones draw during the oral class. But even drawing is not much fun. Mr. Plunkett chooses an object and expects it to be sketched exactly as *he* sees it.

Consequences

Classes finally end. "School, attention!" barks Mr. Plunkett. But no one can go home yet. Now comes Mr. Plunkett's business meeting. "Mary O'Brien," he says, "you will stay late for speaking in class. Jack Johnson, you will stay and clean the classroom to make up for your stupidity. Daniel Brown, you will be responsible for lighting the stove every morning for the next month in order to cure your lateness. Be here before all the other students and see you're not the cause of them freezing to death. And you, Arthur Black, will be whipped the next time I hear of you fighting on the way home from school. The rest of you, go home without delay and make your manners to your parents." (Making one's manners meant bowing for the boys and curtsying for the girls.)

Class dismissed!

"Arrange your desks," continues Mr. Plunkett. The students hurriedly tidy their books and slates.

"Ready!" calls Mr. Plunkett. All is completely quiet.

"Rise!" Everyone rises at once.

"March! One, two, three, four, one, two, three ..."

At five o'clock, Peter and Dorothy arrive home, eat supper, and are soon put to work helping Mother and Father with chores.

Billy practices copying his letters late into the night. He wants to learn to read and write well. He hopes to own a store in town when he grows up. He must be able to read, write, and do arithmetic to be a good storekeeper. The burned-down candles, bottom left, are proof that he works hard to fulfill his ambitions.

From A to Z

Children sometimes learned the alphabet by reading rhymes. In this poem, the two words in *italics* in each line are *synonyms*. Synonyms are words that have the same meaning. Using this poem, children not only learned the alphabet, but they also learned the meanings of difficult words.

A is in *always*, but not in *ever*;
It is in *part*, but not in *sever*.

B is in *bind*, but not in *tie*;
It is in *bawl*, but not in *cry*.

C is in *certain*, but not in *sure*;
It is in *clean*, but not in *pure*.

D is in *din*, but not in *noise*;
It is in *lads*, but not in *boys*.

E is in *evil*, but not in *bad*;
It is in *grieved*, but not in *sad*.

F is in *fountain*, but not in *spring*;
It is in *fetch*, but not in *bring*.

G is in *gladness*, but not in *joy*;
It is in *plaything*, but not in *toy*.

H is in *hue*, but not in *tinge*;
It is in *scorch*, but not in *singe*.

I is in *incense*, but not in *enrage*;
It is in *wise*, but not in *sage*.

J is in *juicy*, but not in *sappy*;
It is in *joyous*, but not in *happy*.

K is in *keep*, but not in *retain*;
It is in *killed*, but not in *slain*.

L is in *lance*, but not in *spear*;
It is in *lake*, but not in *mere*.

M is in *meet*, but not in *fit*;
It is in *wisdom*, but not in *wit*.

N is in *naughty*, but not in *bad*;
It is in *maniac*, but not in *mad*.

O is in *odor*, but not in *scent*;
It is in *bowed*, but not in *bent*.

P is in *prophet*, but not in *seer*;
It is in *precious*, but not in *dear*.

Q is in *quiver*, but not in *shake*;
It is in *quench*, but not in *slake*.

R is in *rapine*, but not in *pillage*;
It is in *culture*, but not in *tillage*.

S is in *sewer*, but not in *drain*;
It is in *suffering*, but not in *pain*.

T is in *twelve*, but not in *dozen*;
It is in *cheat*, but not in *cozen*.

U is in *utter*, but not in *speak*;
It is in *summit*, but not in *peak*.

V is in *view*, but not in *scene*;
It is in *verdant*, but not in *green*.

W is in *wed*, but not in *marry*;
It is in *wait*, but not in *tarry*.

Y is in *yawn*, but not in *gape*;
It is in *monkey*, but not in *ape*.

Z is in *zebra*, but not in *horse*;
It is in *furze*, but not in *gorse*.

Notice that there is no rhyme for words spelled with "x".

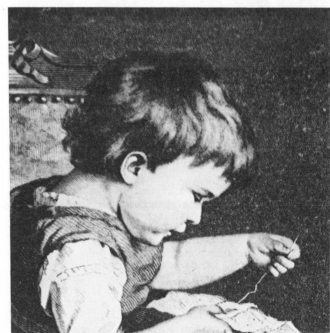

Stitching a sampler was a popular way for girls to test both their sewing skills and knowledge of the alphabet. The finished sampler was proudly hung on the wall at home and admired by visitors. Girls stitched the alphabet in capital and small letters. They also added little verses, their names, their ages, and their hometowns. The border of the sampler was often decorated with trees, flowers, animals, and people.

The girls in this class are practicing their handwriting. They take writing seriously. In those days, how one wrote was more important than what one wrote. People judged compositions by handwriting, not by the imagination that had gone into them.

The art of writing

Children in the early schools wrote much better than children of the same age today. It was more important to be able to write beautifully than it was to be able to spell correctly. The handwriting of the teachers had to be excellent too. If they could not form fancy letters, then they would not get jobs!

The students began by learning how to draw straight lines. They would fill a whole page with them. The better students copied "hooks and trammels." The hook and trammel design was named after the hooks and trammels on which pots were hung in the kitchen. The best students copied sentences which taught them a moral lesson as well as a writing lesson. The moral lesson might have been "Procrastination is the thief of time."

At the end of the school year the pupils wrote special compositions using their best handwriting. The compositions were shown off to visitors. The students decorated the borders of their papers with designs. The visitors admired the handwriting more than they admired the compositions on spring or happiness or friendship!

Writing creatively

Children learned to write stories and poetry in composition class. Here is a poem that was written by a young girl. The teacher thought it was so good that it was sent to a magazine and was printed for everyone to read.

The stream

A tiny river ripples onward,
Babbles over moss and stone,
Flowing, flowing, ever flowing,
Singing in a joyous tone.

Gladly nod the dewy grasses
On its bonny banks and green;
Gladly grow the river mosses,
Peeping little stones between.

Gladly talk the little children,
As they look upon the stream;
Gladly smiles the dancing sunlight,
While the brook reflects its gleam.

Flow, thou happy little river,
Bear thy message night and day,
Telling how the sunny-hearted
Carry sunshine on their way.

In later days, children read from separate readers, as shown in the picture above. Each child in this old picture is reading the same story out loud.

The first readers

The first reader for the settler children was the Bible. Often it was the only book the family owned. If a family could afford it, they would also buy a reader. One reader would be passed from the oldest down to the youngest in the family. The book would become very old and worn.

In many classes, different children had different books. One might have the old reader her father had used, and another might have a new one. It was hard for the teacher and the students to read together from different books.

In later days children read from readers that were suited to their abilities. Most primary schools had four readers. Two grades read from each reader.

"What are you doing in reading, Polly?" asked her aunt.

"Wishing I was home," answered Polly.

110   *THIRD READER.*

9. "Oh, master," cried Carl, "I was looking for something bright when I came upon this poor dove. Some cruel boys were throwing stones at it, and I caught it up quickly and ran here. Oh, I am afraid it will die!"

The old readers did not just teach reading. Each story had a moral or lesson for the children to learn at the same time. It was like killing two birds with one stone.

Each year students had to memorize several hundred lines of poetry or prose from the Bible, a reader, or some famous book. Horace delivers his oration beautifully. He is a born public speaker. Jacob, on the other hand, forgot half of the poem he was supposed to recite. As punishment, he must balance on a block of wood. If he falls off, he will be punished again.

Pro-nun-see-a-shun!

Pronunciation was almost as important as handwriting. Children often read aloud to the teacher. This sample from an old schoolbook is supposed to show children how to pronounce words. It certainly would not teach them to spell!

"The art ov swimming depends furst on keeping the arms and hands undur watur; in protruding only the fase and part ov the hed out ov the water; and then uzing sutsh akshun, as wil derekt the boddy in enny partikulur korse."

Learning words the fun way

We are little airy creatures,
All of different voice and features:
One of us in *glass* is set,
One of us you'll find in *jet*;
The other you may see in *tin*,
And the fourth a *box* within;
If the fifth you should pursue,
It can never fly from *you*.

Answer: Vowels

Picture writing

One of the oldest ways for children to learn reading was with *rebuses* or picture-stories. Here is an example of an old rebus. Can you read it?

The [owl] and the pussy [cat] went 2 C
[house] a beau-[ring]-[wizard]P green [pea]
They II * some [honey] & plenty of [money]
Wrapped up in a 5 [£] [music notes]
The [bird] looked up 2 the [stars] above
And sang II a small [guitar]
O lovely [cat]-y O [cat]-y my love
w-[hat] a beau-[ring]-[elf] [cat]-y UR
UR
UR
w-[hat] a beaut-[eye]-[jester] [cat]-y UR.

Clap or hiss

Half the class leaves the room. While the students are absent, the others decide on a verb that the absent ones must guess and perform. When the verb is chosen, the leader of the party outside is called in by the other students. They say, "The verb we have chosen for you rhymes with *pie*" (for example). The leader goes out and discusses with his or her followers what the verb could be. Let's say that their guess is *buy*. The party enters the room and the students mime the act of buying. If their guess is right (that is, if the verb *to buy* was chosen), the spectators clap their hands. If their guess is wrong, the spectators hiss. Any side that speaks gets a penalty. If they are hissed, the actors leave to discuss another choice. They might decide on *cry, dye, sigh,* and then *fly*. They act out all these rhymes in turn. Finally the other team claps to announce the right choice. When the right guess has been made, the groups switch and the other half of the class gets to act.

Buzz, buzz

Before there were newspapers and telephones, most of the village news was spread by gossip. One person told a story to another person. The second person either added something to the story or took something away from it. The second person told the third person. The third person also changed the story slightly to make it more exciting. Before long, the story was not at all like the original story had been.

The settler children played a game which was similar to the act of gossiping. The teacher whispered a sentence to the pupil in the first seat. That student then whispered the sentence to the next in the row. The whispering continued until the very last student had heard it. The sentence was then repeated by the last student. When the sentence was said out loud, it usually had very little to do with the first sentence. Both the original words and meaning had been lost in the buzz. Try this game in your classroom. What does it tell you about stories passed on by word of mouth? What does it teach you about fact and fiction? Why is this a useful word game?

LESSON VII.   13

bird   It is

a bird   Is it

The girl sees a bird.
It is a black bird.
The girl sees a nest.
Is the bird on the nest?
The black bird is on the nest.
I see a cat. Is it white?
It is a black cat.
The cat sees the bird on the nest.

Is the bird black?

This sample from an 1885 reader shows how spelling, reading, and handwriting were taught in the "new" way.

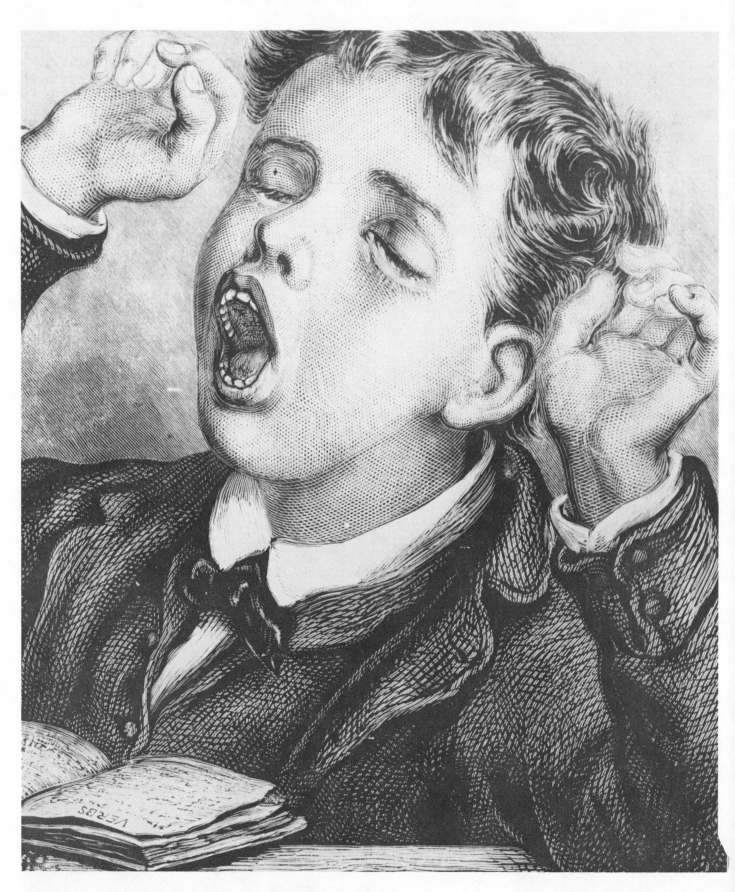

Grammar makes me sick. Verbs make me yawn. Spelling I love, from dawn till next dawn.

Spell crazy

In the early days the ability to spell was not as important as the ability to form beautiful letters. When teachers began to pay attention to spelling, the subject suddenly became very important. The person who could spell best in the school became second only to the student who was best at arithmetic. In some schools, there was a prize for the best speller each day. The prize might have been a coin with a hole drilled through it. It was strung on a necklace. The best speller was allowed to wear it until the next day. At the end of the year, the best speller in the school was given the coin to keep.

Schools held spelling matches. The class was divided into two teams. The pupils competed against each other individually and in teams. One team stood against one wall. The other team stood against the opposite wall. Each student was asked to spell a word. If the word was spelled incorrectly, that child had to sit down. The team with the last standing student or students won the match. The very last person left standing on the winning team was the individual winner. The match often lasted for half the afternoon. It was a noisy event, with the students cheering and boasting.

The spelling craze spread throughout the community. On winter evenings, neighboring districts had their best spellers compete. Everyone came to watch and support a team. After the match, children recited poetry and sang songs.

Sample spelling lessons

Below are two samples taken from old spelling books. Children learned new words by reading them in story form. The stories in the old readers and spellers always had morals to teach as well as new words. The first story ended with the sentence, "And now he goes about the streets begging his bread." The second story had a similar message but from a more positive viewpoint.

1. "I will tell you about the *laziest* boy you ever heard of. He was *idle* about *everything*. When he had spelled a word, he *drawled* out one syllable after another, as if he were *afraid* the syllables would *quarrel* if he did not keep them a great way *apart*. Once, when he was reciting a lesson in geography, his teacher asked him, 'What is said of Milan?' He answered, 'Milan is a flourishing, comical town.' He meant it was a 'flourishing, *commercial* town,' but he never knew what he was about."

2. "Good children will not lie, swear, or steal. They will be good at home, and ask to read their books. When they get up, they will wash their hands and faces. They will comb their hair. They will make haste to school. They will not play on the way as bad boys and girls do."

Which letter am I?

'Tis in *church*, but not in *steeple*;
'Tis in *parson*, but not in *people*;
'Tis in *oyster*, but not in *shell*;
'Tis in *clapper*, but not in *bell*.

(Answer: the letter R)

Grandpa admires the medal Betty won for being the top speller in her school.

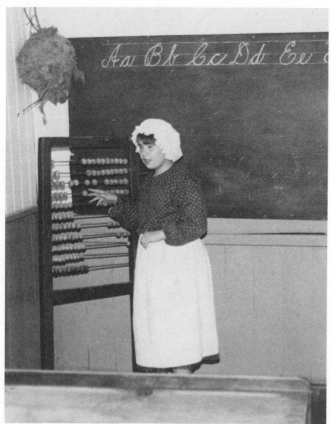

The teacher uses his pocket watch to teach his students how to tell time.

Tamara practices counting by threes on the abacus after school. She wants to beat the teacher in the counting race tomorrow.

"Reckoning" and counting

Arithmetic will teach us how
To reckon and to count;
And when we buy or when we sell,
To learn the right amount.

Notation writes the numbers down,
Numeration does the reading,
Addition sums the *parts* all up,
Gives the *amount* we're needing.

Subtraction will the *difference*
Between the numbers show;
For *minuends* minus *subtrahends*
Remainders leave, you know.

The *multiplicand* and *multiplier*
Are *factors* to be involved
In an answer called the *product*
When by *multiplication* solved.

In *division* write the *dividend*
Then divide by the *divisor*,
And the *quotient* is the answer
That will make the student wiser.

The abacus race

Children began to learn arithmetic by doing simple sums, just as they do today. They often used an *abacus* to learn number value. An abacus was a frame with rows of beads on metal rods or wires. The beads were counted as the teacher flicked them from one end of the wire to the other. Sometimes she moved two or three or five at a time to teach counting by multiples. It was a race to see if the teacher could flick faster than the students could count!

In higher grades the students were given tables of addition, subtraction, multiplication, and division. There were pages and pages of these tables to memorize.

Some teachers, however, did try to make arithmetic more interesting by giving their students poems, problems, and puzzlers about numbers. Try some of these and see if the arithmetic your great-grandparents learned makes sense to you.

Number tricks and teasers

How can you take away one from nineteen, and have twenty remain?

Answer: 0Z = XX ⅋ 6I = XIX

What is the difference between twice twenty-five and twice five and twenty?

Answer: (30 − 50) 20 si rewsna ehT
2 x 25 = 50; 2 x 5 + 20 = 30

How can you divide twelve and end up with two sevens?

Answer: (IIΛ) sneves owt = ƎⅩ ;ZI = IIX

I'd rather be riding

Before trying to solve the problem in this poem, there are three things you should know:

1. The "Rule of Three" is the nineteenth century rule for finding equivalent fractions. If three numbers are given in proportion, one can easily find the fourth.
2. The settlers used miles as their measure of distance.
3. "Fifty" refers to minutes, not hours. A horse could not go fifty hours in a row.

What's the use of the Rule of Three
I should very much like to know?
"If a horse can go twenty miles in two
 hours,
In fifty how far can he go? "

I've tried it this way, I've tried it that,
And it will not come right today;
Oh, if I'd a horse I would saddle him
 now,
And wouldn't I ride away?

Away, away through the shady lanes
And the woods that I love the best;
My horse and I would not heed the time –
We would gallop, then stop to rest.

We would linger along the river bank,
And drink of the cooling tide;
Then canter away through the meadows
green,
And over the blue hills I would ride!

But oh! but oh! what an idle dream!
And the clock is striking one,
And the master says that here I must
stay
Till this horrid sum is done.

A vexing subject

Multiplication is vexation,
Division is as bad;
The Rule of Three it puzzles me,
And practice drives me mad!

'Well, Lucy,' said Anna, 'I'll do what
 I can,
But, my darling, you really should try
To give your whole heart to your work,
 for I know
You're as able to do it as I.

'Now repeat after me: 2 and 1 they
 make 3,
3 and 2 they make 5 and no more;
Add 1 to the 5, and of course you'll
 have 6,
Subtract 2, and then you'll have? – 4.'

27

Some parents objected to sending their children to school. They felt that children should know how to work on a farm. The teacher at this old country school combined reading, writing, and arithmetic with some practical lessons. These children are also learning how to grow flowers, vegetables, and fruit. Their parents are happy with the education the children are getting, even if the children do not seem too thrilled.

Beyond the "three Rs"

Younger children attended school during the summer months. The older students went during the rest of the year. It is a beautiful day. The teachers decided that the best way to learn about science was from Mother Nature herself!

Jack has to draw a picture of his house as a homework assignment. He does it with a slate pencil. He would like to draw his room inside the house. However, he knows he is allowed to draw only what he sees from the outside. That is what Mr. Wilson has asked for.

Children learned geography by memorizing names of countries, cities, lakes and rivers. Ellie is more fortunate than most children. Her father was able to afford this big globe to help his daughter in her studies. Ellie shows her mother where the Atlantic Ocean is.

The Lang children are practicing their do-re-mes. Their schoolteacher, Mr. Gerard also teaches music in his spare time. He is coming to give a singing lesson tonight. Arnold makes sure that his brother and sister can hit the right notes on cue. Mr. Gerard is just as strict when he teaches music as he is when he teaches at school.

Sewing was part of the school curriculum for girls. It was important that girls could make their own clothes. They were also expected to sew clothes for the other family members. Connie is sewing a vest for her brother. She has trouble threading the needle with her chubby little fingers.

Teddy Mullen is proud of the model of the family homestead he made at school. He brought it home as a gift for his sick sister. His mother thinks he has done a wonderful job. He used mud to make the ground, real branches for the bushes and trees, and pieces of paper and wood for the house and fence.

Snap-the-whip was a favorite recess game. The children held hands in a long line. They ran very fast. The first ones in the line stopped suddenly and yanked the others sideways. The ones at the other end were thrown from their feet – they could not hold on. The two children on the left have fallen after the two on the right "snapped the whip."

Instead of playing ball, Irma decides to draw a horse on the school wall. Perhaps her children will see the drawing there some day.

Hurrah! It's recess!

Children were allowed a recess in the morning. In the winter, they often played *Fox and Goose*. The children cleared a big circle in the snow by shuffling their feet. They would then clear six or eight lines going into the center of the circle. The snow design looked like a wheel with spokes. The person chosen to be the "fox" would stand at the very center. The "geese" would run in one direction around the outside ring. The "fox" could catch one of the "geese" by running down one of the paths which went from the center to the outside. The "goose" which had been caught then became the new "fox."

"Ante, ante, over the shanty"

Another game was *Ante, ante, over the shanty*. A ball was the "ante." The school was the "shanty." The ante was thrown over the shanty. The first person to find the ante was the winner of the game.

Magnifying glasses were called "burning" glasses. Harold shows his friends how he can use the sun and the glass to burn a hole in his hat. His little experiment cost him his hat – not to mention the five recesses his teacher made him spend indoors.

Fred was trying to study grammar during recess. Robert, the school joker, decided to play a trick on his friend. Both boys had to stay after school; Robert, for putting the frog down Fred's neck, and Fred, for giving Robert a black eye.

Play while you play

Work while you work, and play while you play,
That is the way to be cheerful and gay;
All that you do, do with your might,
Things done by halves are never done right.

One thing at once, and that one well,
Is a good rule, as wise men tell;
Moments are useless trifled away –
Work while you work, and play while you play!

William, Joe, and Dick made a see-saw from a fat log and a long piece of board. Dick stands in the center to hold the board in place.

See-saw, Margery Daw.

There were many problems with education in the early one-room schools. Below are just a few of them.

There must be better ways to learn!

Some schools were open only for a few months each year. The rest of the time children worked at home.

A teacher could not teach all the students at the same time because they were in different grades. They had to wait their turns.

Some students were older than the teacher. They soon learned all the teacher had to teach.

The bigger students could not fit their long legs under the desks. The smaller students had to dangle their legs from the high benches.

Often the teacher was too busy to think of interesting ways to teach. Many classes were devoted to reciting or memorizing.

Even art class was boring. Students had to draw objects on a slate exactly as the teacher told them to.

The teacher did not tell exciting stories about people in history. Students memorized names and dates instead.

Children marched to and from their desks. This was the only exercise they had. There was no gym class.

Discipline was harsh in many schools. Children had to stand in corners, wear dunce caps, balance on blocks of wood, and wear signs tied around their necks. Many teachers also gave the strap.

Dash to school

Jack is growing very old,
Summers six have seen his joy;
Mother may no longer hold
In her arms so big a boy.
He must go to school, I know,
Through the world his ship must steer:
How that little heart of his
Beats with mingled pride and fear!

Kiss him, or his heart will fail;
Dash looks up with gleaming eye,
By the wagging of his tail
Marks his doggish sympathy.
Jack attempting to be cool,
Whispers with an eager sigh,
"If I might take Dash to school
I believe I should not cry."

Jack is happy that Dash followed him to school. The other children enjoyed the unexpected excitement of having a dog in class.

Well educated women in the larger towns took girls in and taught them basics, such as how to spin, weave, knit, and embroider. These girls were also taught to read and write. However, academic subjects were not the main part of their day. This old picture shows that the classroom is not furnished with desks. The room contains spinning wheels and

They called themselves "teachers"

Before there were local schoolhouses, some parents sent their children to the nearest town to board at the home of a doctor or minister. These professionals made extra money by teaching the children after they had finished their regular work. In some areas, churches opened schools. Some church schools were private. Others were charity schools for poor children.

Strict nannies

Wealthier settlers sometimes brought governesses over from England or Europe. Governesses lived with the families they worked for. They taught the children to read and write, and to behave politely. The job of a governess was often much like the job of a babysitter.

Hitting the wrong target

Girls from wealthy families were sometimes sent to board with educated women in the towns. They were taught how to sew, embroider, write, and dance. They were taught good manners. They were even taught how to walk straight with books balanced on their heads! In one case a miller sent his daughter to board with a lady he thought was "genteel." To his surprise and horror, his daughter did not learn how to read, sew, or write. She learned to shoot a target while riding a horse. And she could hit the target from almost any distance!

looms. These girls were taught by two sisters who believed that girls should know everything about running a home and raising a family.

The governess warns Molly that if she runs or falls down she will have to do an extra lesson in spelling. Judging by Molly's dress, she has already broken the rule that one must walk gracefully.

Traveling teachers

Some of the teachers who came to the New World could not find permanent jobs. They traveled around the countryside and boarded with different families. During their stay with a family they taught the children in the home. Then they moved on to another household and taught new children. They received room and board and a little money in return for teaching. These teachers were called *itinerant* teachers. They made their rounds from house to house. After several months, they returned to the house where they had begun their travels.

Apprenticeships

Parents of poor children often could not afford to send their children to school. Some of these children were lucky enough to get apprenticeships with millers, black-smiths, or other craftspeople. Some children were only seven years old when they started apprenticeships.

Many boys were educated by ministers. Parents felt ministers made good teachers because ministers were well educated. Girls were also sent to board out. They were usually sent to convents. They were taught to read, write, do arithmetic, sew, knit, and show good manners. The eight girls in this old photograph have two "sisters" as their teachers.

The many jobs of the teacher

The settlers hired a teacher as soon as they decided to build a school. Sometimes a teacher offered to teach in a village, and then the villagers decided to build the school. The first teachers were usually men. Some teachers wandered from place to place and taught at a new school each year. Others became members of a community.

When a teacher was hired, he usually boarded with families in the area. He lived with one family for a few months and then moved on to the next house.

The teacher's job included more than teaching. He might visit the sick and read to the blind. He might ring the church bell on Sundays and read the sermon at the church service. He was even the gravedigger in a few cases.

The sacrifice of the schoolmaster

It had been a terrible winter. Snow kept falling in a sheet of dazzling white until it rose high over fences. Travelers were sometimes lost in the whirling drifts just before they reached their homes. Many a farmer, searching for his stray cattle, lost his life trying to save them.

There happened at this time to be a young English teacher at the school. He was a serious young man, but he had a gentle heart and an unselfish nature. His name was Philip Strickland. His brother thought he was wasting his time at a small school. But Philip shook his head. "I like the work," he said. "If I gave it up, no one would take it because the pay is so small. Besides, I am engaged to marry a girl here. Leave me in peace."

But Philip and the girl he was to marry had a big argument. She had another admirer. With a bitter heart, Philip gave himself up more than ever to the work of his little school.

Meanwhile, a snowstorm had begun. One day in January only seven boys and two girls came to school. Their love for the teacher was so strong that they could not be kept at home. It was a terrible day. As the afternoon went on, it became clear to the master that his young flock must stay overnight. The fire was piled high with logs. The children were fed. Philip, giving up his bedroom to the two little girls, camped down with the boys in the classroom.

The dangerous journey

Next morning the snow was still falling. For three days it was the same. The schoolhouse was blocked up. The pantry was empty. Philip decided to make his way to the general store to bring back food. It was a difficult trip and he was almost dead when he finally reached the store. He was fed and warmed, but he refused to stay. "May God protect him," said the storekeeper to his wife, as Philip set off.

Philip Strickland visits one of his sick pupils. He had a very kind heart.

Philip strays from the path

Philip was toiling up a hill when suddenly he heard a dog howl. He knew the creature's master must be near, so he left the path to find him. The dog led him to a mound of snow. Underneath was Bill, the man Myra was now going to marry. Philip lifted Bill onto his sled and pulled him to Myra's home. Then he prepared to leave again, worried about the children. "Don't be a fool. Stay the night," said Myra's father. But Philip refused to listen. "I must go," he said. Myra wept bitterly.

Two days later the sky cleared. Two men, whose children were at the school, made their way to the back door. Nine white faces met them. "Thank the Lord! Our children are safe," said one of the men. "But where is the schoolmaster?" "Teacher went to get food and hasn't come back," said one child.

Two days later they found the schoolmaster's body. He had lost his way. His face was calm and peaceful, and on a page of his pocketbook he had written these words: "Food for the children. Quick."

Mr. Taylor was not strict enough for this bunch!

No rewards for kindness

Many communities wanted to hire men as teachers for one important reason. Teachers were expected to teach their students morals and behavior. Parents felt that the only way to teach children to behave properly was by strict punishment. Teachers were expected to beat children. Parents thought that men would be more able to do this than women.

Punishments for bad behavior were often cruel. Harsh teachers whipped the soles of the students' feet. They forced children to stand in front of the class wearing dunce caps. One teacher seemed to enjoy heating his leather strap and wetting the hands of his pupils. When the strap was hot and the hands were wet, the punishment was particularly painful.

If a teacher was not able to discipline his class, "putting out" was sometimes the result. The following story is about a teacher whose kindness was not returned by his pupils.

A "ruff" education

Mr. Taylor had been hired to teach at Ruffstone School because he read the Bible so beautifully and mended pens so perfectly. Mr. Taylor was only twenty years old. He was small in size.

The boys in his class were just the opposite. They were huge and very mean. A few of them were almost as old as Mr. Taylor. Ruffstone School was known for being "hard." "Hard" was a word people used to describe a school where the boys "put out" teachers. The teacher who had taught before Mr. Taylor had been "put out" of the school and run out of town by the boys.

The boys did not learn their lessons in class, but they taught the other children how to cause trouble. One morning the students came early with their lunch pails full of something. They went into the schoolhouse and stood at the door and windows. They saw Mr. Taylor arrive and walk up to the door. He came in.

Shots in the dark

Suddenly the room was pitch dark, and poor Mr. Taylor was pelted with cold, melting snowballs. He could not see a thing. He could only feel the snow as it hit him and began to melt on his clothes. The students had shut the door and blocked the windows with their coats so that no light could come into the room. When Mr. Taylor finally stumbled to the door to let the light in, all of his pupils were sitting quietly at their desks.

Run out of town

Mr. Taylor did not know what to do. He panicked. He ran from the room. The children shouted and scrambled after him, throwing snowballs at the teacher as they ran him out of town.

Is might right?

The next teacher at Ruffstone School was twice the size of Mr. Taylor. He was not as good at mending pens. However, he knew how to put the big boys in their place. He was the meanest teacher the school had ever known. The boys were sorry they had not given poor Mr. Taylor a chance to teach them something other than how to get the strap.

A teacher's prayer

I want to teach my students how
  To live this life on earth
To face its struggles and its strife
  And to improve their worth
Not just the lesson in a book
  Or how the rivers flow
But how to choose the proper path
  Wherever they may go
To understand eternal truth
  And know the right from wrong
And gather all the beauty of
  A flower and a song
For if I help the world to grow
  In wisdom and in grace
Then I shall feel that I have won
  And I have filled my place
And so I ask Your guidance, God
  That I may do my part
For character and confidence
  And happiness of heart.

It was difficult for a woman to get a teaching job. Most settlers were afraid that a woman could not discipline the children as a man could. They felt that physical punishment was the best punishment. Female teachers usually had to teach the smaller students in the summer months. The older students were taught by a man during the rest of the year. People did not realize that challenging children with interesting lessons was the answer to having a well-behaved class.

Most of the young female teachers quit teaching after they married. In those days, most married women were not allowed to teach. A few women preferred to teach rather than to marry. Mrs. Smith has taught for many years. Sometimes even she finds her lessons a touch boring!

Equal opportunities for women?

A woman who wanted to teach had to have an excellent moral character. If she was not known for her record of good behavior then it did not matter how well she was educated. It was difficult for a woman to get a job in a strange town. People preferred to hire someone they knew.

There was not much a male teacher could do wrong, but a female teacher was watched closely. In one instance a young teacher, Kate Henderson, was called in by the board of trustees to defend her teaching methods. The board of trustees was made up of the storekeeper, the miller, the minister, and the doctor. Rumors were spreading through the village that Miss Henderson was "in league with the devil."

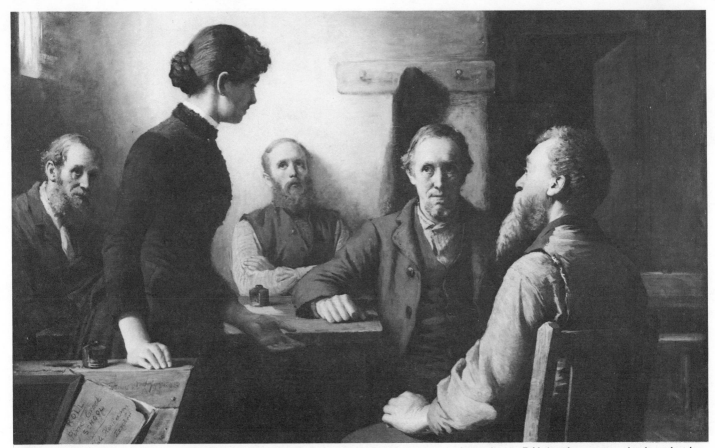

Miss Henderson had a hard time convincing the trustees that her Bible lessons helped the children to understand the word of God.

Kate defends her ideas

Teaching the Bible was one of Miss Henderson's duties at Pine Creek School. Her younger students learned the Scriptures but did not understand them. One day Miss Henderson had an idea. She decided to ask her students to act out a Scripture passage. Her students loved the experience of acting. It was like the game of "pretend" that they played at home. They went home that day full of happy news about school. Many parents were shocked. They wanted Miss Henderson fired. They called a meeting of the school board. They felt that it was sinful to pretend to be people from the Bible. It was making fun of the Word of God, they said.

So Miss Henderson was called in by the trustees. They asked if she had anything to say in her defense. She tried to explain that it was useless for children to learn Bible verses if they did not know what they meant.

The Reverend has a plan

Miss Henderson was told not to go to the school for a week. In the meantime, the board would meet to discuss the case. Reverend Goodleigh, the young minister, could not find anything wrong in her actions. In fact, he had noticed how excited the children had been in church the Sunday before. They were quite interested in what he had to say. He told the other members of the board that he had to think about his decision. He would not be hasty in voting to fire the teacher.

The meaningful Word

Reverend Goodleigh had a plan. On the following Sunday he asked some of his smallest parishioners to act out the story of the Prodigal Son. His sermon that day was about new ways to understand the Word of God. By the time the service was over, the whole community realized what Miss Henderson had tried to do. She had helped the children to realize the meaning of God's Word. Without meaning, the words had been nothing but empty sounds to the children.

Miss Henderson did not lose her job. She is still remembered as one of the finest teachers Pine Creek School ever had.

Mr. Cosgrove spends his evening whittling pens for the students in his class. He lives with the Richards family. Mrs. Richards approves of the way the teacher spends his extra time.

Rules for teachers

There were strict rules about what duties a teacher had to fulfill. A teacher was expected to behave properly at all times. Here are some rules that teachers had to obey in the year 1872.

1. Teachers will fill the lamps and clean the chimney each day.
2. Each teacher will bring a bucket of water and a scuttle of coal for the day's session.
3. Make your pens carefully. You may whittle nibs to the individual tastes of the pupils.
4. Men teachers may take one evening each week for courting purposes, or two evenings a week if they go to church regularly.
5. After ten hours in school, the teachers may spend the remaining time reading the Bible or other good books.
6. Women teachers who marry or engage in improper conduct will be dismissed.
7. Every teacher should lay aside from each day's pay a goodly sum of his earnings. He should use his savings during his retirement years so that he will not become a burden on society.
8. Any teacher who smokes, uses liquor in any form, visits pool halls or public halls, or gets shaved in a barber shop, will give good reasons for people to suspect his worth, intentions, and honesty.
9. The teacher who performs his labor faithfully and without fault for five years will be given an increase of twenty-five cents per week in his pay.

Mr. Hartley reminds his students to "make their manners" to their parents when they reach home. Boys were expected to bow and girls to curtsy. Children were taught to respect their elders.

Rules for students

Good students in early schools were expected to earn more than high marks. There were many rules to follow and duties to perform. The schoolmaster really was the "master" of his pupils. Children were told to obey the master of the school even if obedience meant having to stand still while being strapped. Here are some rules for students.

1. Respect your schoolmaster. Obey him and accept his punishments.
2. Do not call your classmates names or fight with them. Love and help each other.
3. Never make noises or disturb your neighbors as they work.
4. Be silent during classes. Do not talk unless it is absolutely necessary.
5. Do not leave your seat without permission.
6. No more than one student at a time may go to the washroom.
7. At the end of the class, wash your hands and face. Wash your feet if they are bare.
8. Bring firewood into the classroom for the stove whenever the teacher tells you to.
9. Go quietly in and out of the classroom.
10. If the master calls your name after class, straighten the benches and tables. Sweep the room, dust, and leave everything tidy.

Many reasons for missing school

Johnny dawdles to school.

Children missed school more often than they do today. Some parents, and some children, believed that the work to be done at home was more important than schoolwork. The books could wait, but the weeds would choke the garden and the crops would not be harvested if the children did not help at home.

Problems within the family also kept children home from school. If Mother fell ill, the daughter or son might be needed to look after her and the younger children. If Father became sick, the oldest child might have to find work to support the family. And even when everyone was healthy, some families were too poor to buy schoolbooks for the children.

Some children did not feel it was necessary to attend classes regularly. Why study when you planned to get a job that required a strong body rather than brains? Even after people began to feel that education was very important, however, there were still truants. Children thought they had better things to do! In this poem, Johnny really has nothing better to do except waste his time.

Johnny Dawdle

Here, little folks, listen, I'll tell you a
  tale –
Though to shock and surprise you I fear
  it won't fail;
Of Master Dawdle my story must be,
Who, I'm sorry to say, is related to me.

And yet, after all, he's a nice little
  fellow –
His eyes are dark brown, and his hair
  is pale yellow;
And, though not very clever, or tall, it
  is true,
He is better than many, if worse than
  a few!

But he dawdles at breakfast, he dawdles
  at tea,
He's the greatest small dawdle that ever
  could be;
And when in his bedroom, it is his delight,
To dawdle in dressing at morning and
  night.

44

Sleeping over "sums"

And, oh! if you saw him sit over a sum,
You'd much wish to pinch him with finger
    and thumb;
And then if you scold him, he looks up
    so meek;
Dear me! one would think that he hardly
    could speak.

Each morning the same he comes tumbling
    down,
And often enough is received with a
    frown,
And a terrible warning of something
    severe,
Unless on the morrow he sooner appear.

But where does he live? that I'd rather
    not say,
Though, if truth must be told, I have
    met him today,
I meant just to pass him with merely a
    bow,
But he stopped and conversed for a
    minute or so.

"Well, where are you going?" politely
    said I,
To which he replied, with a groan and
    a sigh,
"I've been doing my sums from breakfast
    till dinner,
And pretty hard work that is for a
    beginner."

"But now I suppose you are going to
    play,
And have pleasure and fun for the rest
    of the day."
"Indeed but I'm not, there's that
    bothering sum;
And then there's a tiresome old copy
    to come."

"Dear me!" I replied, and I thought it
    quite sad
There should be such hard work for one
    poor little lad;
But just at that moment a lady passed by,
And her words soon made clear that
    mistaken was I.

Late for school

"Now then, Mr. Dawdle, get out of my
    way,
I suppose you intended to stop here all
    day;

The bell has done ringing, and yet, I
    declare,
Your hands are not washed, nor yet
    brushed is your hair."

"Oh ho!" I exclaimed, "Mr. Dawdle,
    indeed,"
And I took myself off with all possible
    speed;
Quite distressed that I should for a
    moment be seen,
With one who so lazy and careless had
    been.

So now if you please, we will wish him
    goodbye;
And if you should meet him by chance,
    as did I,
Just bid him good morning, and say that
    a friend,
(Only don't mention names), hopes he
    soon may amend.

Must I go to school?

"Oh, Father! Must I go to school?" said
Oliver one morning, as his mother was
getting him ready. "I don't understand
books. I never will. I would rather cut
wood in the bush with you, and work
terribly hard."

"Oliver, how did we fell that big tree
yesterday?" asked his father.

"With one stroke at a time, and by keeping
at it," answered the boy.

"Exactly so," said his father. "A word at
a time, and keeping at it, will make you a
good reader. A syllable at a time, and
keeping at it, will make you a good speller.
A sum at a time, and keeping at it, will
make you good in figures. A thought at a
time, and keeping at it, will make you
master the hardest book in the world. By
patiently keeping at it, Oliver, you will be
a scholar."

"Is that all?" asked Oliver.

"All," said his father.

"I know that I can do that," said Oliver.
Six years later, he stood first in the
highest class in school.

These boys all had to sit on the dunce's bench. In the old days, if a child could not answer a question correctly, he or she was called a "dunce." In some classrooms, the teacher even had dunce caps for the children to wear. These boys are not given the extra help from their teacher which would help them understand their lessons. They are ignored. They fall further and further behind in their studies. They begin to misbehave or fall asleep because they are too bored to do anything else.

Punishment

David was late today. He must stay after school. His little friends are all going home as he sits sadly on the bench. He will probably have to clean the blackboard and pick up garbage in the school yard. Morris gives him a sympathetic glance before he leaves for home.

Caught in the act! Lionel has changed the face of the clock to resemble the face of his teacher. The other boys shudder to think of the punishment Lionel will receive. Perhaps he will be beaten. He might even be locked into the "dungeon." The dungeon was a dark closet in the cellar reserved for those who had misbehaved. It usually contained a rat or two.

One did not fall asleep in class! Stephen was caught napping by his angry teacher. He is in for a rude awakening. Mr. Allen raises his leather glove above Stephen's head. He will surely deliver a stinging blow to the boy's left ear. Another teacher punished his sleeping students by burning their bare ankles with a magnifying glass. Both teachers might have asked themselves whether their boring lessons caused snoozing in class.

Receiving a note from the teacher was a serious business, as shown by the old joke below.

"Well, Carter, have you been punished at school lately?" asked his uncle.

"Oh, no, sir," replied Carter, "The teacher sends a note to Papa, and he sees to it at home."

A teacher today might think of this as a good joke. However, this teacher can not. She is furious. She feels her students are being "disrespectful." If she finds out who built this snow image, the guilty ones will surely suffer for their work of art.

Children learned lessons in school that were supposed to "build their character." This schoolmaster teaches his students the "five-finger lesson." In the "five-finger lesson" pupils were taught five characteristics: truthfulness, honesty, punctuality, cleanliness, and kindness.

Manners and morals

Schoolmasters and schoolmarms taught their students lessons about behavior as well as lessons from school books. "Character building" was an important part of a teacher's job. The teacher taught children how to behave at home as well as at school. Parents might wonder whether the teacher had good manners if their sons did not take off their hats in the house or if their daughters did not speak to them with respect. Teachers were blamed for the bad manners of their students. In fact, the teacher's lessons simply wore off as soon as the pupils left the school! The following list of words shows the characteristics that students were expected to turn into habits: punctuality, industry, truthfulness, neatness, honesty, courtesy, self-control, generosity, and kindness.

Here is a story from an old children's magazine. Do you think this lesson should have been taught at school?

The five-finger lesson

Passing by the village school, I decided to enter, and heard the schoolmaster give the following lesson.

"Now, children, I am about to speak about the virtues and happiness of life, and in doing so I shall use your fingers to impress it upon your memories. I shall call it 'the five-finger lesson,' not only because you use your fingers, but also because you will always have the lesson at your fingertips.

"Now then, to begin. Hold the left hand up and spread the fingers out. Take the forefinger of the right hand, and touch the thumb of the left. Say 'one.'

Truthfulness

1. "*Speak the truth*. We must begin with that. There is no getting on without a love of truth. Do not allow others to be mistaken about you. If you have something to say, say the truth out boldly. Do not be afraid of the consequences of telling the truth. Remember that. Now, put the first finger from the thumb onto the first finger of the left hand. Say 'two.'

Honesty

2. "*Be honest*. Now, to be honest is to be real. It is not to let the outside look smart when the inside is not so. You should remember that if you do not work as hard and as steadily when no one is looking as you do when someone is - then you are dishonest. Now to the middle finger. Say 'three.'

Punctuality

3. "*Be punctual*. Remember, if you are late, you will make others late if they wait for you. You must learn to be punctual. Lord Nelson, the great admiral, said that always being five minutes early made him what he was. On to the next finger. Say 'four.'

Cleanliness

4. "*Be clean*. Cleanliness is next to godliness. Always be fit to be seen. Your room should be clean and neat so that you never have to blush if someone comes in unexpectedly. Be moderate in eating and drinking. Always stop when you have had enough. Now to the little finger. 'Five.'

Kindness

5. "*Be kind*. You can change the worst character by being kind. Be firm in not giving up what you know is right, but be kind. If you are, you must succeed in the end.

"And now I hope you will try your hardest to keep these good resolutions. If you do, you will feel when you go to bed at night that your five-finger lesson has been truly valuable to you throughout the day."

"Making one's manners"

Children were often told by their teachers to "make their manners." To make her manners, a girl curtsied. To make his manners, a boy bowed. Some teachers settled for a nod of the head from both boys and girls. Other teachers called their students to the front of the classroom every morning. Then the students made their manners to the teacher.

At recess the children had to make their manners to any strangers or neighbors who passed by the school. If an important person in the community passed by, such as the minister, all the children had to line up and curtsy or bow together. At the end of each day the teacher told the students to make their manners to their parents when they arrived home.

Mary has "made her manners" to the teacher by curtsying. She offers him a bouquet of wildflowers. Children were told to "make their manners" to any adults they met.

Photographs, such as the one above, bring back memories of the one-room schoolhouses.

Good old golden rule days

In the following stories, people who attended one-room schools share some of their memories with us.

Barefooting!

"When I was about seven years old, my father had to go past the school in the morning with the team of horses. We wanted to ride with him, but I could not find my shoes. I went to school barefooted. When school let out, there was an inch of hail on the ground. I ran home two and a half miles - barefooted. I made good time!"

The rat trap

"There was a hole in the school wall so wide that rats came into the room. The teacher made a trapdoor with a string attached to his desk to keep it open. A rat would poke its nose through and then come into the room. The teacher would release the trapdoor and all the children would join in the chase. Some of them climbed on the desks and benches and screamed. The teacher and the braver students, armed with brooms and sticks, shouted and stamped with all their might. The poor rat!"

So there!

"During Mr. Green's last year at the school, he gave us a test in geography. I had not done enough work to suit him. He accused me of not working. I told him I *had* worked. I was told to stay in at recess. At recess he was writing on the blackboard. All at once he turned around and asked me if I thought my word was as good as his. I told him my word was as good as anybody's. He came down and thrashed me and made me go back a grade."

Christmas Eve at the old school was the biggest event of the year for the students. Even Saint Nick came to give out gifts.

Christmas at the old schoolhouse

"We were preparing for Christmas Eve at the schoolhouse. It was the biggest event of the school year. The school was decorated with pine and spruce boughs. It smelled lovely! The boys had brought in a gigantic pine from the bush. It was covered with popcorn strings and homemade toys.

The canned dress

"My sister, Gertie, was getting a new dress from my aunt. She wanted to look her very best for the Christmas concert. She went to pick it up. It had beautiful lace ruffles. Gertie was quite pleased with herself and rather vain. My aunt asked her to take home a milk can. It was the day before the Christmas Eve concert. The milk can was almost as big as Gertie, but it was empty and not very heavy. In order to carry her dress and the can, Gertie put the lacy thing into the can. She forgot all about it. The next morning, in went the milk. The dress did not make a sound!

How could Mother have known? The mistake was found out and Gertie was punished for her carelessness. She did not even care, however, for when the dress was washed, it looked as good as new.

Even Saint Nick showed up

"That night, the parents poured into our little schoolhouse. They all came, young and old, to watch the plays and listen to the speeches and songs. Between the decorations and the people, there was no room except on the stage. Even Saint Nick showed up. Everything was perfect. One of the best parts, of course, was the food. All the mothers baked and brought something delicious.

"When we returned to the same old schoolhouse in January, there was no trace of that magic night. But the memory of Christmas at the schoolhouse was with me then and is with me now."

Life at boarding school

Children from "well-to-do" families were often sent to private schools or boarding schools. They were expensive. The children lived at the school. Here is their daily routine:

6:00	rise	1:30	study
6:30	morning	4:15	recreation
	prayers	4:30	study
7:15	breakfast	5:45	dinner
8:00	study	8:00	study
10:45	recreation	9:00	evening
11:00	study		prayers
12:15	lunch	10:00	bed

The boarding school students had a long, hard day. They made fun (and trouble) whenever they had a chance. Follow the pictures on these pages. They tell a story of what happened one day and night at a boarding school.

1 *Mark receives a huge cake in the mail. His mother often sends him goodies because he complains about the boarding school's food.*

2 *Mark greedily kept the cake all to himself and did not offer to share it with the other boys. They plan revenge. During lunch break they steal the master's keys.*

3 *Daniel gets into the linen closet with the stolen key. He steals a sheet and "borrows" the kitchen broom from the cook. He creates a ghost.*

4 *The boys decide a "real" ghost would be much more frightening. Daniel volunteers for the job. The ghost appears just as Mark takes his last bite of cake. He nearly chokes. He leaps out of the room.*

5 *The noise has awakened the schoolmaster. He is furious as he heads for the boys' dormitory with his candle.*

6 *The boys are wide awake and howling over their joke. In comes the schoolmaster. Into bed jump the boys!*

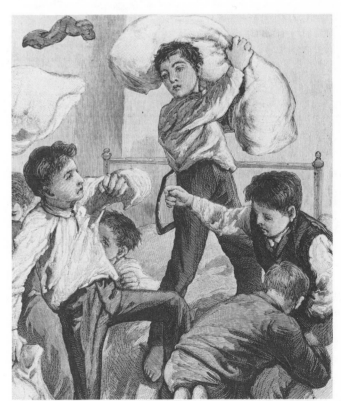

7 *Mark does not forget his fright. As the boys are dressing for classes, he attacks Daniel with his pillow. All the boys join in. After the fun is over, Mark promises his friends that he will share his next cake with them.*

Annie tries to cheer up her two roommates. Most of the girls will be spending Christmas away from their families. Some of them are more homesick than others. In those days children were not given long Christmas holidays. Many schools were open even on Christmas day!

The early education of girls

At first, many girls did not have the same kind of schooling as boys did. Some people thought that it did not make sense to teach girls mathematics and science because their jobs would be to look after their homes and families. Girls were taught to read and write, but sewing lessons were considered more useful than science classes.

In some areas, girls went to school only in the short summer season. Boys went to school in the winter. In some areas, the boys went home early so the girls could come to school late in the afternoon. Boys and girls were sometimes taught separately because people thought the rough behavior of some of the boys would be a bad example to the girls!

Ideas about the education of girls changed gradually. People began to understand that girls should have the same classes as boys. They realized that girls should be trained for careers outside the home as well as in the home.

Finishing schools

The first schools for girls who had completed primary school were called "finishing schools." The girls lived at the school. They learned French, dancing, embroidery, and manners. These lessons were supposed to "finish" or polish off a girl's education. People thought that acquiring these skills would help a girl to lead a happy and successful adult life.

In the following letters, Annie, who is away at a finishing school, writes to her sister. Annie's letters describe life at one of these schools.

Feeling homesick

Darling Rosie:

Only two days before Christmas! How can I ever keep from being homesick? My two roommates have been sad and homesick too. On Christmas day, we will probably have no more than a half day for a holiday.

My studies are enjoyable. French is fairly easy now, but it is hard to find time to do all my work. I am sewing a large sampler and learning gymnastics. But oh! I sometimes wish we could study a little astronomy or chemistry!

Well, darling sister, I must close this short letter. I will write after Christmas day. I think of you all the time. My love to Mamma, and a merry, merry Christmas from,

your loving sister,
Annie

Christmas away from home

Darling Rosie:

Christmas has come and gone, and at last I have time to write you to tell how the day went. Mamma's and your letters came to me on Christmas Eve. I was so delighted to get them.

We had a whole day of holiday for Christmas. We all had a sleigh ride. In the afternoon our class practiced gymnastics for the visitors. We also played games and listened to music. My French teacher sent us little books bound in brown leather which he had written himself. Of course the teachers also received gifts. We, the gymnastics class, gave Miss Merton a handsome silver fruit dish, breakfast tray, and a silver spoon. She is to be married soon.

It is so pleasant to have two nice roommates - more so than I thought it would be.

Good night, my darling. My love to Mamma. I shall write to her tomorrow.

Yours lovingly,
Annie

The girls showed off their gymnastics to the visitors on Christmas day.

Rosie is happy to get Annie's letter. She will be attending the same finishing school as her sister next year. She can hardly wait to be with Annie again.

These boys are working hard in the ragged school's woodworking shop. They are making small tables which will be sold at the town's furniture store. These children pay for their food and education with their labor. They learn valuable skills at the same time.

Working and learning at "ragged schools"

In some towns and cities, people started "ragged schools" or industrial schools for poor children. These schools were opened so poor children could get an education. Instead of paying money to go to school, the children paid for their lessons by working at the school. They made shoes, furniture, and clothes. They looked after the school. Children were assigned to serve the food at mealtimes. They did the laundry, chopped the firewood, and swept the floors. Some ragged schools were miserable places. Others were pleasant, however, because they were run by kind people.

Here is a letter from a girl at a boarding school to her mother. The mother can afford to send her daughter to the boarding school, but she also runs a ragged school for children who cannot afford to go. Her daughter, Elsie, describes a ragged school she has been reading about.

Dear Mamma,

So you are starting up another ragged school. I hope you will succeed. Of course you will. I have been reading a book about ragged schools. In one case, some kind people hired rooms and a teacher. Then they told the poor children that they could come and get food, work, and lessons. They offered four hours of lessons, five hours of work, and three good meals a day. No child could eat meals if he or she had not been at work or lessons. In this way, attendance was better than at ordinary schools. The work that the children did, such as carpentry and sewing, helped to pay for the school.

The school does not promise to provide clothes for the children, but people often send old clothing. In this way, the poorest children have something to wear. Classes begin at seven o'clock in the winter. The school day begins with reading the Bible, singing, and prayer. The students have lessons in geography and nature study.

While the boys are busy making tables, the girls put in a good day's work sewing and knitting. Hardly anyone missed a day of school. For many poor children the food they ate at school was the only food available to them.

At nine o'clock, they have a breakfast of porridge and milk. Then they have a half hour of play. At ten o'clock they start work. They continue until two o'clock, and then they dine. Dinner is usually thin soup with bread. From dinner until three, their time is spent on exercising or chores. From three to four they work in the garden or workroom. From four until seven they learn reading, writing, and arithmetic. At seven o'clock they have a supper of porridge and milk. After short religious exercises, they are sent home. They attend Saturday and Sunday, but on Sunday they go home after dinner to go to church with their parents. They come back at five, and go home again after supper.

I thought this information might be useful to you. I am working hard at school and remain,

your dutiful daughter,
Elsie

Dinner at the ragged school was served at two o'clock. The children are given a bowl of soup and a slice of bread.

Boys at this trade school learn to work with iron. This job can be dangerous because one has to use a torch to heat the iron before the design can be completed.

Cutting wood correctly is a complicated task. The boy in this class was taught subjects such as geometry and science in order to make the best use of wood.

New schools for new skills

Many things have changed since the building of the earliest one-room school-houses in the country. Now there are many people moving to the cities and towns. The New World is getting older. Companies and businesses want to hire people who have been taught special skills. Schools are beginning to hold special classes to train young people in woodworking, architecture, iron-working, and art. Different kinds of schools have opened to teach young men and women trades.

People have also started to think about the art and science of managing a home. They realize that working in the home is a difficult and demanding job. Domestic science classes are held to teach children to cook, to sew, to keep to a budget, and to care for a family.

The girls in this domestic science class are taught to run a household efficiently. In cooking class, they learn the science of nutrition as well as how to prepare food.

As towns grew into cities, more and more buildings were needed. These children began to learn about design when they were young. Some of them will become architects.

More schooling for a better society

Sooner or later people realized the importance of educating their children. This old drawing appeared on the cover of an 1873 newspaper. It showed how education would open new doors to the future.

There was a new interest in education in the last half of the nineteenth century. Parents knew that not all their children would grow up to live in the country or to become farmers. Parents realized the importance of school. The work of the future would present challenges different from those faced by the early settlers. The challenges could not be met without the training provided by a good education.

A good system of education meant having good teachers. Colleges for teachers opened all over the country. Teachers now had to know more than their students! They had to teach lessons in more interesting ways. They had to find out what made children want to learn.

The government made education compulsory. That meant that every child had to go to school from the age of six to the age of fourteen. These children are in the first grade. They love school. Today they made a necklace which they display proudly.

Do your best

Do your best, your very best,
And do it every day;
Little boys and little girls,
That is the wisest way.

Whatever work comes to your hand,
At home, or at your school,
Do your best with right good will;
It is a golden rule.

Still do your best, if but at taw
You join the merry ring;
Or if you play at battledore;
Or if you skip, or swing.

Or if you write your copybook,
Or if you read or spell,
Or if you seam, or hem, or knit, -
Be sure you do it well.

Glossary

academic *the opposite of practical or technical*

account *a written record of what a person bought and how much it cost*

apprenticeship *the fixed amount of time a person must spend working for another person in order to learn a trade or a business*

architecture *the science of designing and constructing buildings*

battledore *a game similar to badminton*

blacksmith *a craftsperson who makes instruments and utensils out of iron*

board of trustees *a group of people chosen to say how a school should be run*

bonny *beautiful*

career *job; occupation*

chilblains *swellings on the hands or feet caused by cold*

community *a group of people who live together in one area, who have the same needs and interests*

consequence *effect; result*

contract *an agreement between two or more people, often written down*

convent *a religious community, especially of nuns*

courting *the act of trying to win someone's love*

crossroads *the place where roads meet*

cue *a word, a sign, or an action which signals the start of another speech or action*

culture *the raising of plants or animals*

curriculum *the courses of study offered at a school*

cutter *a small sleigh*

dawdle *to waste time*

discipline *a system of training people to behave in a certain way*

dividend *the number which is to be divided; e.g., in 20 ÷ 10 = 2, "20" is the dividend*

divisor *the number by which another number is divided; e.g., in 20 ÷ 10 = 2, "10" is the divisor*

drill *to teach someone something by repeating it over and over again; a method of teaching*

embroidery *fancy needlework*

enrage *to make someone angry*

erect *to put up a building*

exaggerate *to make something greater in size*

factor *one of two (or more) numbers that, when multiplied together, produce another number; e.g., in 3 x 5 = 15, "3" and "5" are factors*

fell *to cut down*

flattery *things said to someone else to make that other person feel happy, but which are really not meant*

furze *a prickly shrub with yellow flowers*

generation *a group of people born at about the same time*

godliness *the state of being filled with love for God*

gorse *a prickly shrub with yellow flowers*

grammar *the rules for using language*

handiwork *things made by hand*

hue *color*

incense *to make someone angry*

individual *a single human being; a person*

kindling *small pieces of wood with which a fire is started*

land deed *a certificate showing that someone has bought a piece of land*

lard *animal fat; grease*

livestock *farm animals, such as horses, cattle, or sheep*

loom *a machine on which thread is woven into a piece of cloth*

luxury *something that it is wonderful to have, but which is not absolutely necessary for survival*

meet *suitable*

memorize *to learn by heart*

miller *the person who operates a mill, e.g., a gristmill*

mime *to tell something to somebody else, using actions instead of words*

minuend *the number from which another number is to be subtracted; e.g., in 16 − 4 = 12, "16" is the minuend*

moral *to do with the goodness or badness of a person or thing*

multiplicand *a number which is to be multiplied by another number; e.g., in 3 x 5 = 15, "3" is the multiplicand*

multiplier *the number by which another number is multiplied; e.g., in 3 x 5 = 15, "5" is the multiplier*

notation *figures used instead of words to express quantities*

numeration *the act of counting by reading or writing numbers*

nutrition *the way a body takes in and uses food to grow*

pillage *taking in a violent way the money or property of those you are fighting against in a war*

plow *a machine used to break up and turn over the soil*

prodigal *wasteful*

product *the result obtained by multiplication; e.g., in 3 x 5 = 15, "15" is the product*

pronunciation *the way words are said*

prophet *one who says what will happen in the future*

quench *to satisfy (a thirst)*

quill *a pen made from a feather*

quotient *the result obtained by division; e.g., in 20 ÷ 10 = 2, "2" is the quotient*

rapine *taking in a violent way the money or property of those you are fighting against in a war*

recite *to say something from memory*

remainder *the amount that is left after subtraction; e.g., in 16 − 4 = 12, "12" is the remainder*

resolution *a statement of what somebody intends to do*

Saint Nick *Santa Claus*

scorch *to burn slightly*

(from) scratch *from the beginning; from nothing*

scuttle *a metal container for coal*

seer *one who says what will happen in the future*

singe *to burn something slightly*

slake *to satisfy a thirst or an appetite*

slate *a small piece of blackboard*

sophisticated *very fine to look at, or able to do many things* sow *to scatter seed over the land*

spinning *twisting strands of thread together into yarn, such as wool or silk*

strife *fighting*

subtrahend *a number which is subtracted from another number; e.g., in 16 - 4 = 12, "4" is the subtrahend*

summit *the highest part; the top*

syllables *the units of sound a word can be broken up into when it is spoken*

taw *a game of marbles*

tillage *the cultivation of land*

tinge *a faint trace of color*

transparent *something that can be seen through*

trifle *to spend time in a useless way*

truant *somebody who is away from school without permission*

verb *an "action" word; e.g., "think", "give"*

virtue *a quality that people think is very good to have; e.g., honesty, kindness*

volunteer *to offer to give or to do something*

vowels *the letters "a","e","i","o" and "u"*

whittle *to shape something by cutting or shaving bits from it*

Index

Acknowledgements

Library of Congress, Dover Archives, Colonial Williamsburg, Century Village, Lang, Upper Canada Village, Black Creek Pioneer Village, Metropolitan Toronto Library, Colborne Lodge, Toronto Historical Board, Gibson House, City of North York, Dungannon Women's Institute, Harper's Weekly, Notman Photographic Archives, McCord Museum, Canadian Illustrated News, Public Archives of Canada, Ontario Archives, Frank Leslie's Illustrated Magazine, the Osborne Collection of Early Children's Books, Toronto Public Library, the Buffalo and Erie County Public Library Rare Book Department, Jamestown, Chatterbox, Little Wide Awake, Harper's Round Table Magazine, John P. Robarts Library, William Blackwood and Sons, Scarborough Historical Society, Book Society of Canada, Enoch Turner School.

1617181920 LB Printed in the U.S.A. 54321